A Flash

by Frederick James
illustrated by George Ulrich

Practice Decodable 34

McGraw Hill Education

Bothell, WA • Chicago, IL • Columbus, OH • New York, NY

MHEonline.com

Send all inquiries to:
McGraw-Hill Education
8787 Orion Place
Columbus, OH 43240

ISBN: 978-0-02-145355-9
MHID: 0-02-145355-1

Printed in China

8 9 10 11 12 DSS 27 26 25 24 23

It was six. Gramps shut his shrimp shop.

Gramps and Josh sat.
Josh held a shell.

Josh spotted a flash.

"What is the flash?" he asked.

"It helps ships see big rocks," said Gramps.

“It helps the ships not to crash,” Gramps added.

"I am glad the flash helps," said Josh.